W9-DFC-291

SCIENCE OF SPORTS

THE SCIENCE OF HOCKEY

WITH MAX AXIOM

SUPER SCIENTIST

by Blake Hoena

illustrated by Caio Cacau

Consultant:
Lyle A. Ford
Department Chair
Physics & Astronomy
University of Wisconsin, Eau Claire

CAPSTONE PRESS
a capstone imprint

Graphic Library is published by Capstone Press,
1710 Roe Crest Drive, North Mankato, Minnesota 56003
www.capstonepub.com

Library of Congress Cataloging-in-Publication Data
Hoena, B. A.
  The science of hockey with Max Axiom, super scientist / by Blake Hoena.
    pages cm. — (Graphic Library. The Science of Sports with Max Axiom.)
  Includes bibliographical references and index.
  Summary: "Uses graphic novel format to reveal the science at play behind the sport of
hockey"— Provided by publisher.
  ISBN 978-1-4914-6086-3 (library binding)
  ISBN 978-1-4914-6090-0 (paperback)
  ISBN 978-1-4914-6094-8 (eBook PDF)
  1. Hockey—Juvenile literature. 2. Sports sciences—Juvenile literature. 3. Graphic novels—
Juvenile literature. I. Title.
  GV847.25.H65 2016
  796.962—dc23   2015012519

Editor
Mandy Robbins

Designer
Ted Williams

Creative Director
Nathan Gassman

Media Researcher
Jo Miller

Production Specialist
Laura Manthe

Printed in the United States of America in North Mankato, Minnesota.
042015   008823CGF15

TABLE of CONTENTS

SECTION 1

PLAYING AT SUPER SPEED -------4

SECTION 2

SKATING AROUND THE RINK -----10

SECTION 3

MOVING THE PUCK AROUND -----16

SECTION 4

SCORING A GOAL------------------20

SECTION 5

BLOCKING THE SHOT -------------24

Max Axiom and some fellow scientists have put on their ice skates and hockey gear. Their team, the Atoms, will face off against the Beakers.

Time for the starting face-off! Eyes on the puck, gentlemen.

There isn't much to that small, black disk. It's about the size of a hamburger and doesn't weigh much more.

Yet watch what happens when this hunk of rubber is dropped onto the ice.

A hockey game has begun!

Or as I like to think of it: A game of contact chess played at super speed.

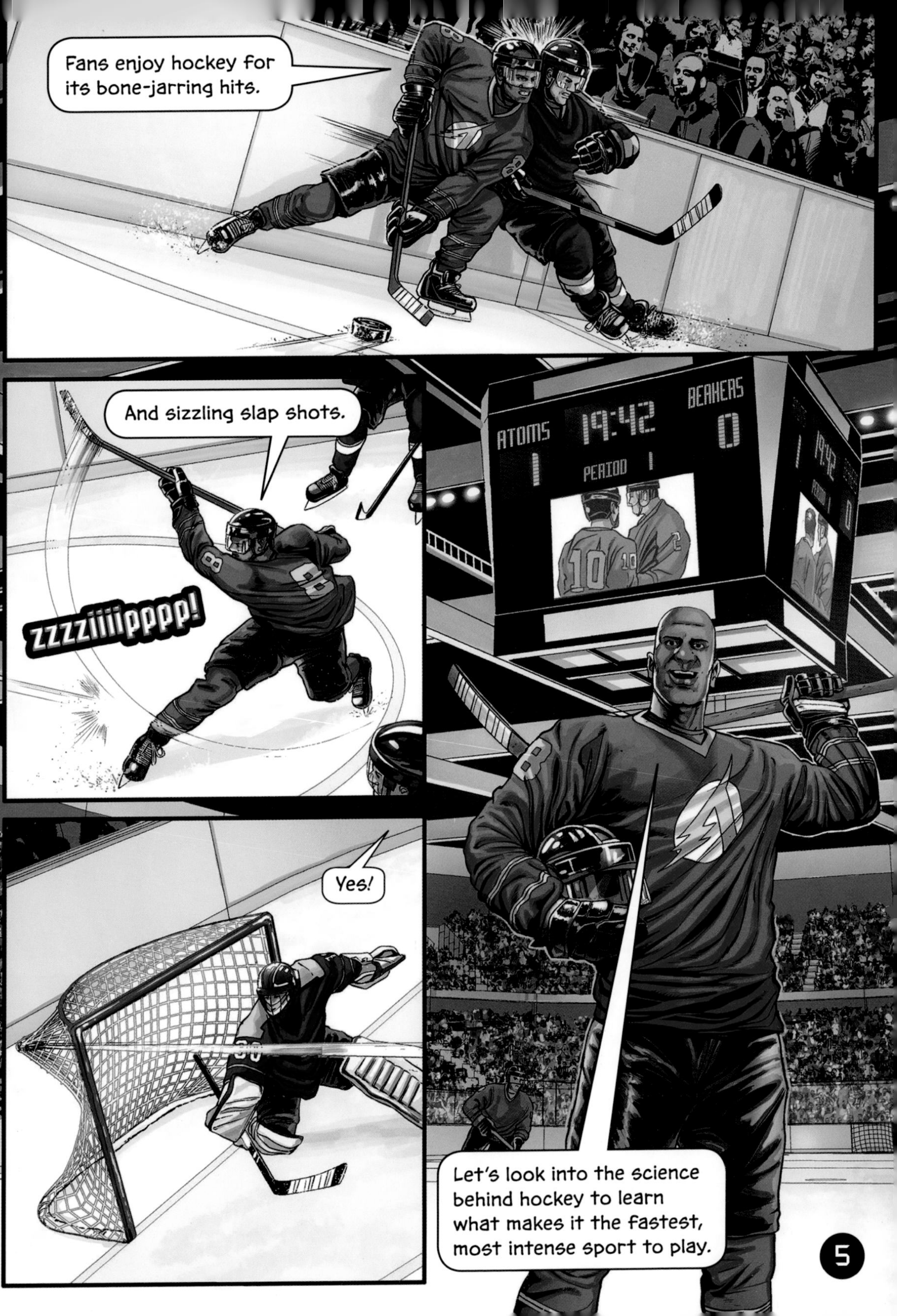
Fans enjoy hockey for its bone-jarring hits.
And sizzling slap shots.
ZZZZiiiiPPPP!
ATOMS 1
19:42
BEAKERS 0
PERIOD 1
Yes!
Let's look into the science behind hockey to learn what makes it the fastest, most intense sport to play.

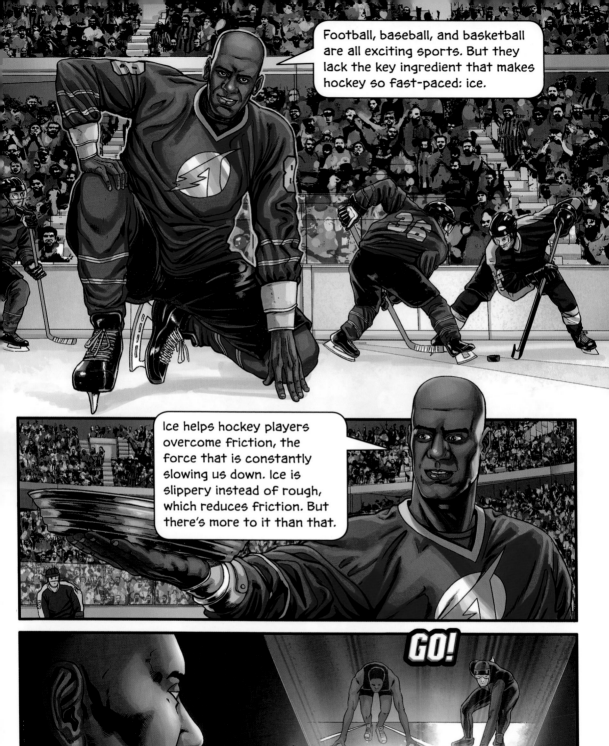

Football, baseball, and basketball are all exciting sports. But they lack the key ingredient that makes hockey so fast-paced: ice.

Ice helps hockey players overcome friction, the force that is constantly slowing us down. Ice is slippery instead of rough, which reduces friction. But there's more to it than that.

GO!

To see what I mean, let's compare a track sprinter and a speed skater.

6

A sprinter pushes off with his back foot. When his lead foot hits the track, the impact of his shoe against the ground creates friction, which slows him.

The greater the impact between two surfaces, the more friction is created.

A speed skater's lead foot slides across the ice. This motion creates less friction, so the skater's forward movement isn't slowed as much.

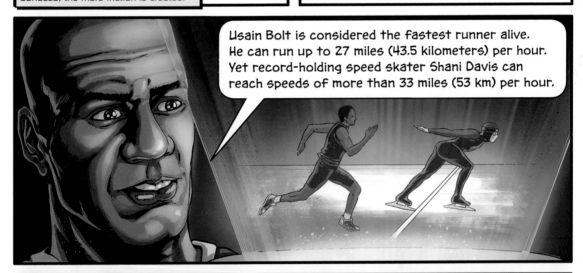

Usain Bolt is considered the fastest runner alive. He can run up to 27 miles (43.5 kilometers) per hour. Yet record-holding speed skater Shani Davis can reach speeds of more than 33 miles (53 km) per hour.

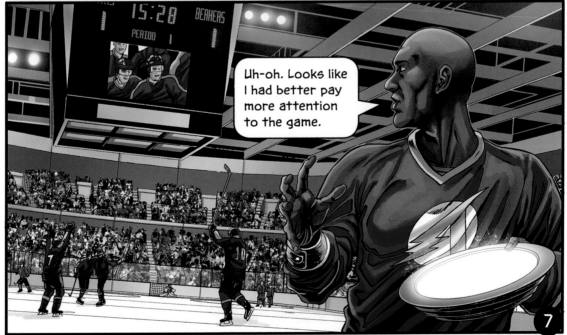

Uh-oh. Looks like I had better pay more attention to the game.

So what's the difference between the surface of a running track and an ice rink? They are both solids.

Ice is simply frozen water. Water turns solid when its temperature drops to 32 degrees Fahrenheit (0 degrees Celsius).

To answer that question, we need to take a much closer look.

But ice has a slippery surface. A hockey puck just slides across it. Why?

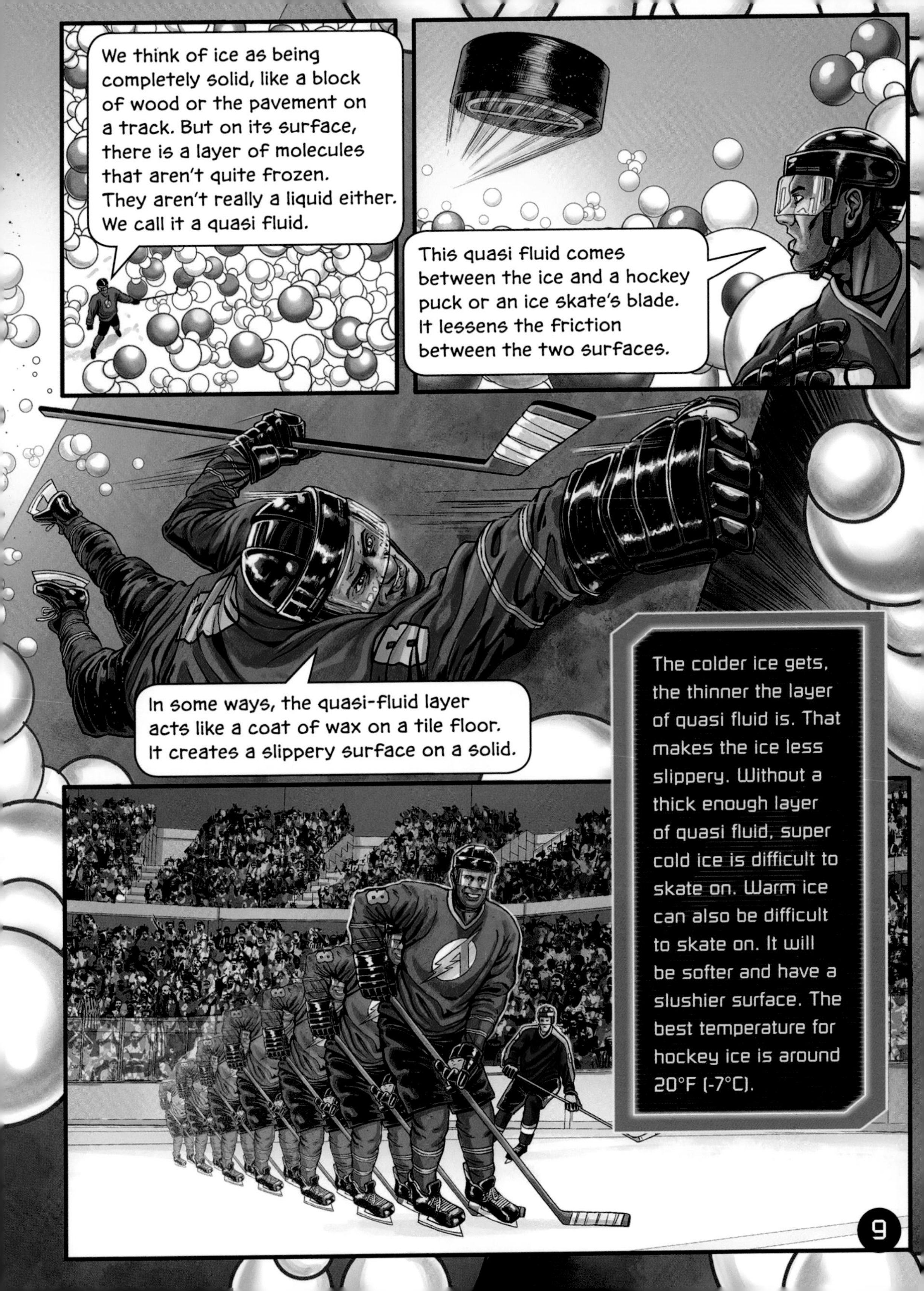
We think of ice as being completely solid, like a block of wood or the pavement on a track. But on its surface, there is a layer of molecules that aren't quite frozen. They aren't really a liquid either. We call it a quasi fluid.
This quasi fluid comes between the ice and a hockey puck or an ice skate's blade. It lessens the friction between the two surfaces.
In some ways, the quasi-fluid layer acts like a coat of wax on a tile floor. It creates a slippery surface on a solid.
The colder ice gets, the thinner the layer of quasi fluid is. That makes the ice less slippery. Without a thick enough layer of quasi fluid, super cold ice is difficult to skate on. Warm ice can also be difficult to skate on. It will be softer and have a slushier surface. The best temperature for hockey ice is around 20°F (-7°C).

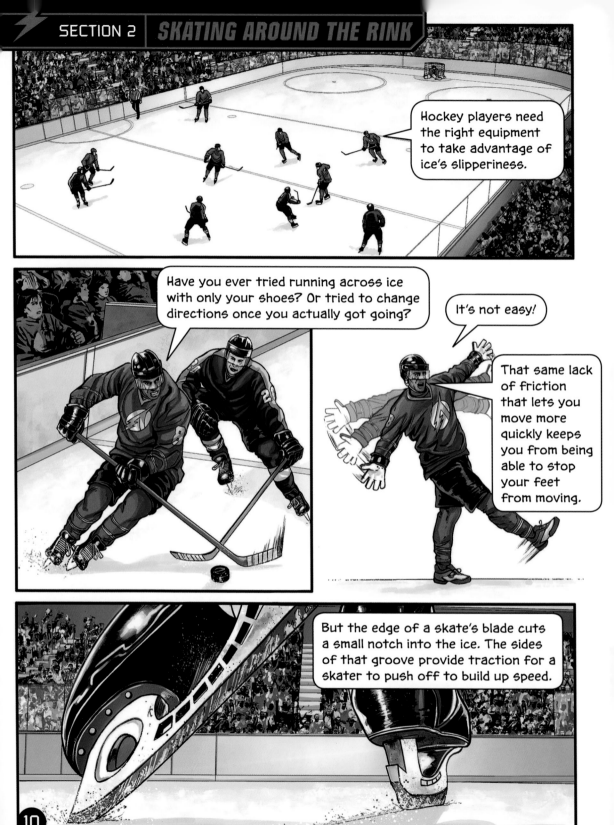

Hockey players need the right equipment to take advantage of ice's slipperiness.

Have you ever tried running across ice with only your shoes? Or tried to change directions once you actually got going?

It's not easy!

That same lack of friction that lets you move more quickly keeps you from being able to stop your feet from moving.

But the edge of a skate's blade cuts a small notch into the ice. The sides of that groove provide traction for a skater to push off to build up speed.

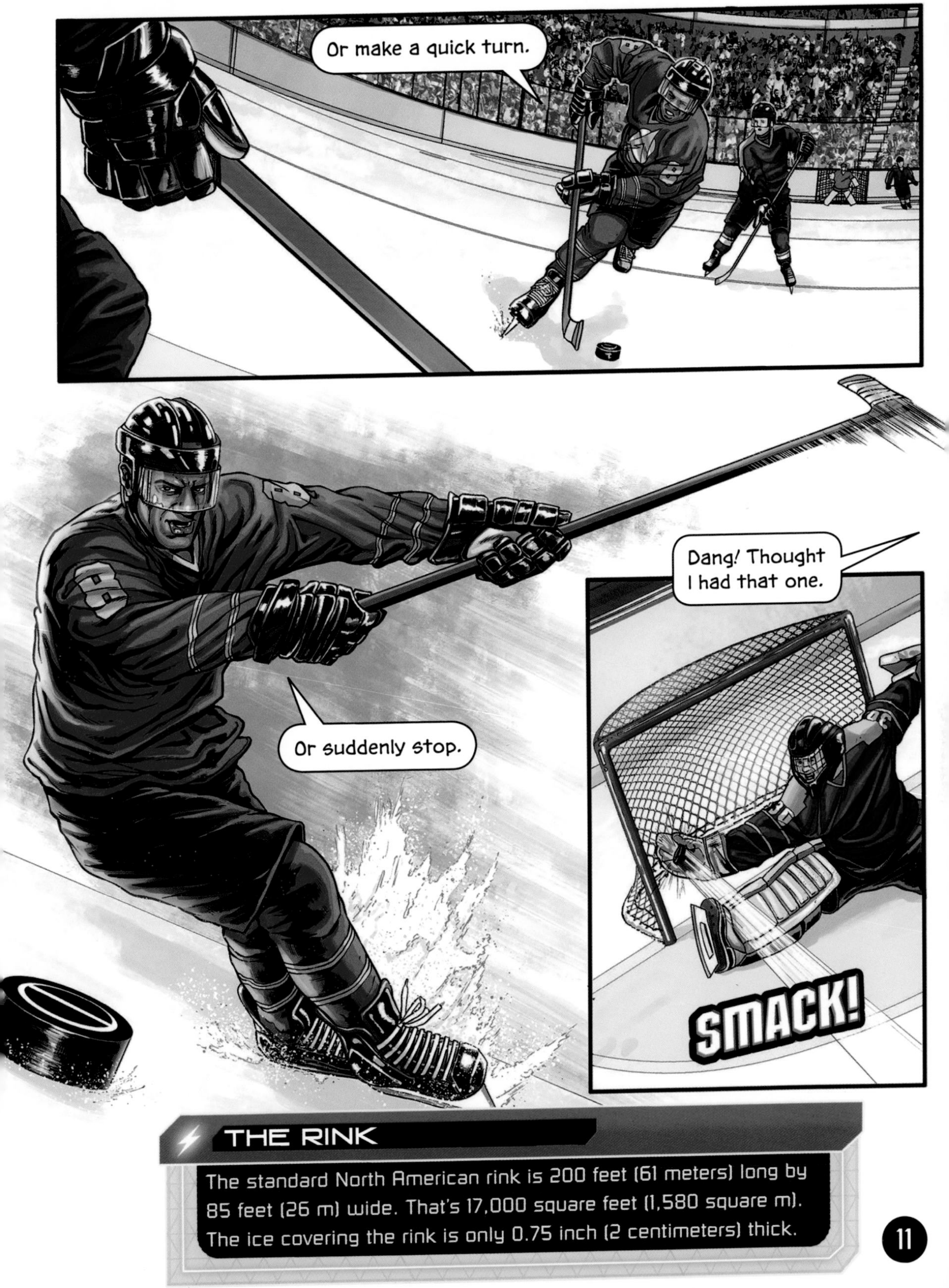
Or make a quick turn.
Or suddenly stop.
Dang! Thought I had that one.
SMACK!

THE RINK

The standard North American rink is 200 feet (61 meters) long by 85 feet (26 m) wide. That's 17,000 square feet (1,580 square m). The ice covering the rink is only 0.75 inch (2 centimeters) thick.

Now mix all that speed with sharp skates and a flying puck, and you have a fast-paced, dangerous game! That's why hockey players wear safety equipment. Safety pads absorb the force of a hit whether it's from the puck, a stick, or another player.

A **HELMET** keeps a player's head safe. A plastic visor or cage protects the face and eyes.

GLOVES do more than keep a player's hands warm! The outsides are heavily padded for protection.

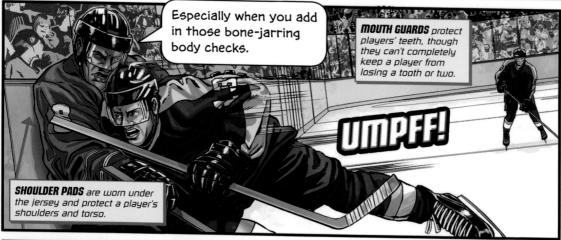

Especially when you add in those bone-jarring body checks.

MOUTH GUARDS protect players' teeth, though they can't completely keep a player from losing a tooth or two.

UMPFF!

SHOULDER PADS are worn under the jersey and protect a player's shoulders and torso.

I'll take that.

ELBOW PADS not only protect a player's elbows, but they cover the upper forearms and lower triceps as well.

SHIN GUARDS cover the knees and protect the shins from getting smacked by swinging hockey sticks.

Take the shot!

SAFETY GLASS protects people who aren't even on the ice. The rink is lined with a wall of clear, shatter-resistent plastic to keep fans safe from flying pucks.

A **NECK GUARD** is made of cut- and puncture-resistant materials. It keeps a player's neck and throat safe from flying pucks and sharp skate blades.

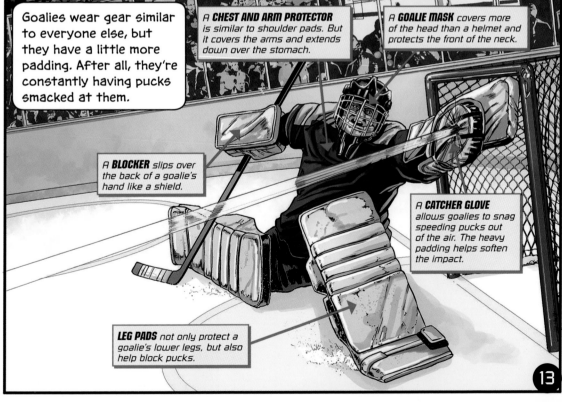

Goalies wear gear similar to everyone else, but they have a little more padding. After all, they're constantly having pucks smacked at them.

A **CHEST AND ARM PROTECTOR** is similar to shoulder pads. But it covers the arms and extends down over the stomach.

A **GOALIE MASK** covers more of the head than a helmet and protects the front of the neck.

A **BLOCKER** slips over the back of a goalie's hand like a shield.

A **CATCHER GLOVE** allows goalies to snag speeding pucks out of the air. The heavy padding helps soften the impact.

LEG PADS not only protect a goalie's lower legs, but also help block pucks.

BUZZZZZ

That's the end of the first period. Get ready for one of my favorite parts of the game. It's Zamboni time!

SNOW TANK—The front, hollow part of the Zamboni ice resurfacing machine can hold more than 1 ton (0.9 metric ton) of snow.

WASH WATER TANK—This tank holds up to 100 gallons (380 liters) of water.

All that pushing off, turning, and stopping with skates roughs up the ice's smooth surface. So between periods, the ice needs to be resurfaced.

Let me pop on my X-ray vision goggles to give you a closer look.

FRESHWATER TANK—This tank holds water heated to around 140°F (60°C).

VACUUM—This part sucks up the dirt and excess water. The dirt is filtered out so the water can be used again in the wash water tank.

BLADE—Toward the back of the machine is a blade that shaves the surface of the ice to help smooth it out.

14

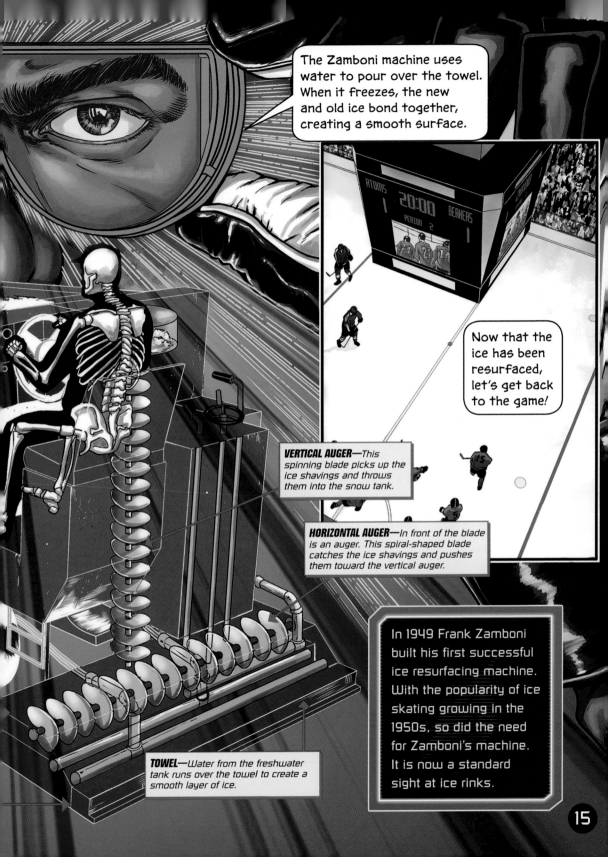

The Zamboni machine uses water to pour over the towel. When it freezes, the new and old ice bond together, creating a smooth surface.

Now that the ice has been resurfaced, let's get back to the game!

VERTICAL AUGER—This spinning blade picks up the ice shavings and throws them into the snow tank.

HORIZONTAL AUGER—In front of the blade is an auger. This spiral-shaped blade catches the ice shavings and pushes them toward the vertical auger.

TOWEL—Water from the freshwater tank runs over the towel to create a smooth layer of ice.

In 1949 Frank Zamboni built his first successful ice resurfacing machine. With the popularity of ice skating growing in the 1950s, so did the need for Zamboni's machine. It is now a standard sight at ice rinks.

SECTION 3 MOVING THE PUCK AROUND

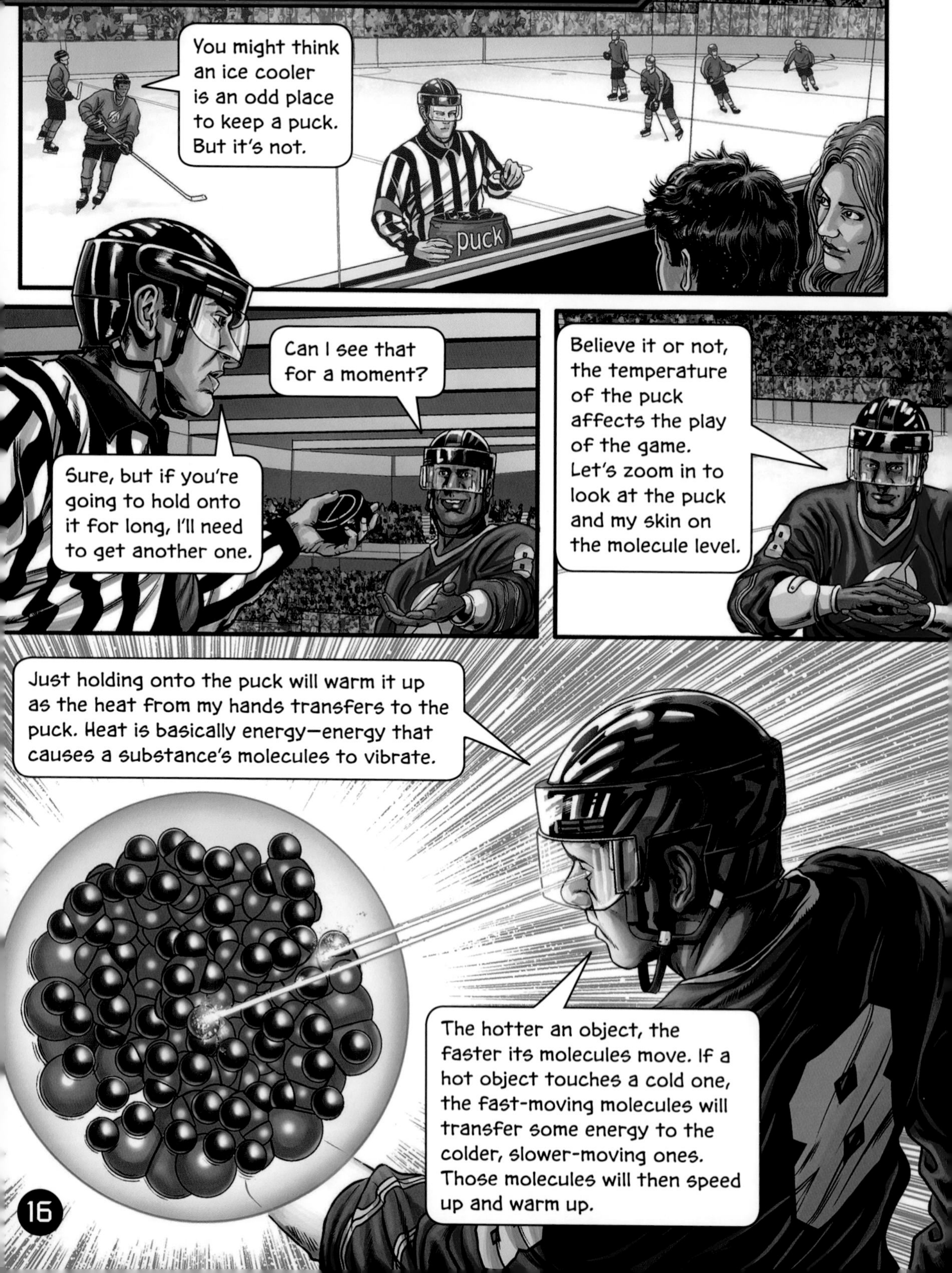

puck
You might think an ice cooler is an odd place to keep a puck. But it's not.
Can I see that for a moment?
Sure, but if you're going to hold onto it for long, I'll need to get another one.
Believe it or not, the temperature of the puck affects the play of the game. Let's zoom in to look at the puck and my skin on the molecule level.
Just holding onto the puck will warm it up as the heat from my hands transfers to the puck. Heat is basically energy—energy that causes a substance's molecules to vibrate.
The hotter an object, the faster its molecules move. If a hot object touches a cold one, the fast-moving molecules will transfer some energy to the colder, slower-moving ones. Those molecules will then speed up and warm up.

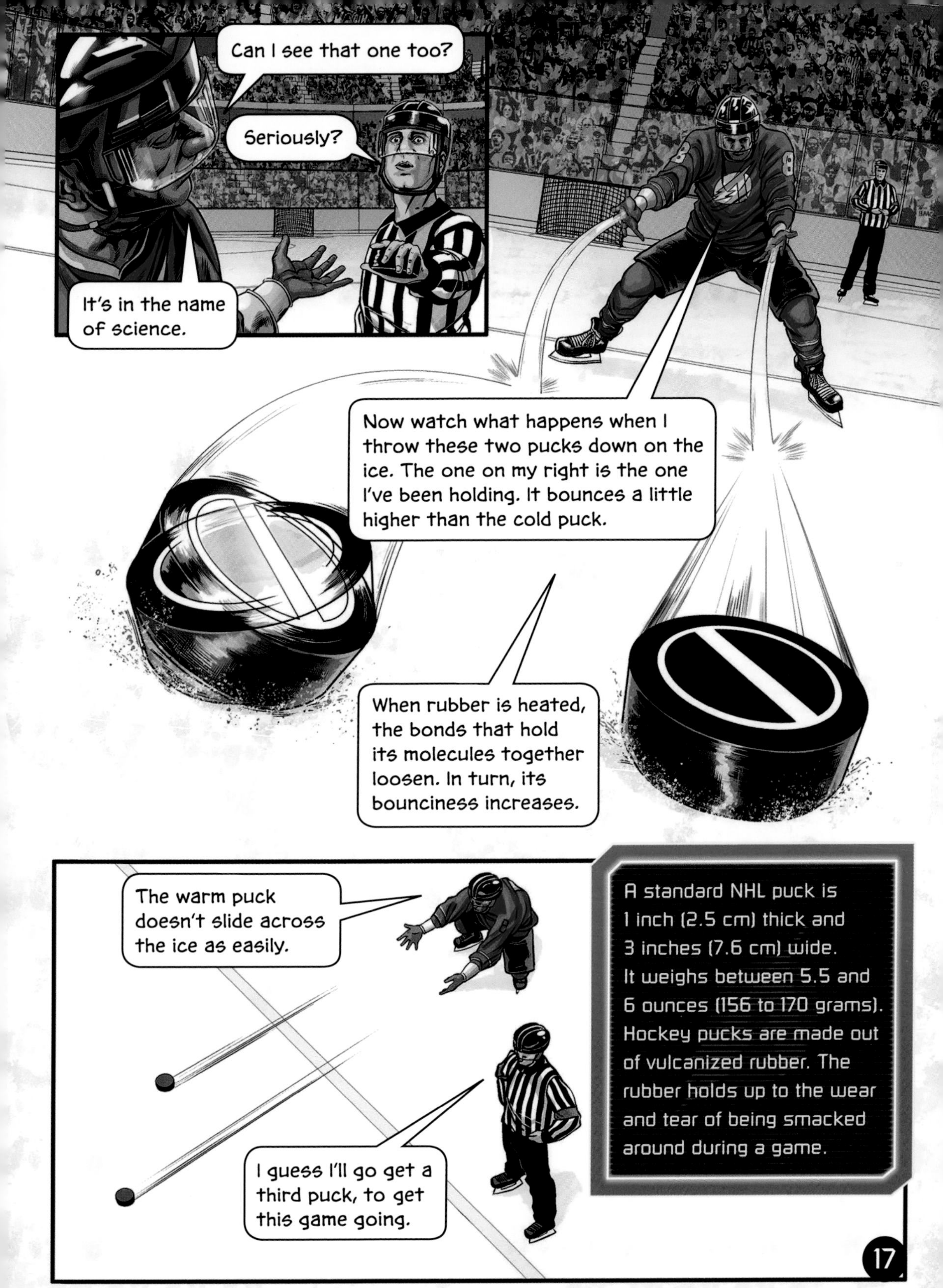
Can I see that one too?
Seriously?
It's in the name of science.
Now watch what happens when I throw these two pucks down on the ice. The one on my right is the one I've been holding. It bounces a little higher than the cold puck.
When rubber is heated, the bonds that hold its molecules together loosen. In turn, its bounciness increases.
The warm puck doesn't slide across the ice as easily.
A standard NHL puck is 1 inch (2.5 cm) thick and 3 inches (7.6 cm) wide. It weighs between 5.5 and 6 ounces (156 to 170 grams). Hockey pucks are made out of vulcanized rubber. The rubber holds up to the wear and tear of being smacked around during a game.
I guess I'll go get a third puck, to get this game going.

A hockey game can't begin until the puck hits the ice. But skates are the key piece of equipment hockey players use to move around on the ice.

Hockey sticks are how players move the puck around.

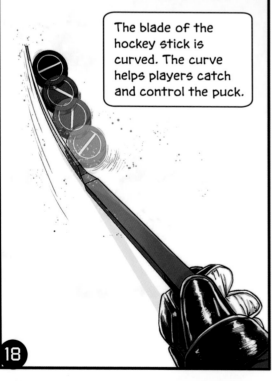

The blade of the hockey stick is curved. The curve helps players catch and control the puck.

The curve also aids in accurate passing, as the curve helps focus the direction of the pass.

Each player's stick is unique to him or her. Some players like to have a curve in the middle or toward the end of the stick. Some players like longer sticks, which provide more power. Others like shorter sticks for better control.

SHAFT—The shaft is the long part of the hockey stick that players hold. It works as a lever to propel the puck across the ice.

LIE—The lie is the angle where the shaft and the blade meet. The lie can vary greatly depending on a hockey player's preference. But the wider the lie, the longer the stick usually is.

BLADE—Not only is the blade curved inward, but the face of the blade is often tilted slightly. The tilt helps loft the puck on those sizzling slap shots.

TAPE—Tape on the blade offers extra friction between the puck and the blade. It helps players maintain better control of the puck.

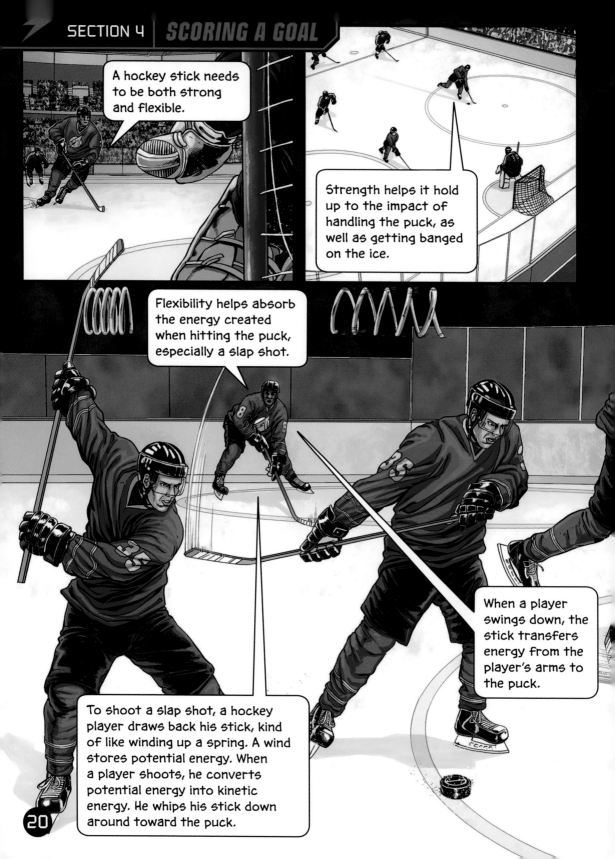

A hockey stick needs to be both strong and flexible.

Strength helps it hold up to the impact of handling the puck, as well as getting banged on the ice.

Flexibility helps absorb the energy created when hitting the puck, especially a slap shot.

When a player swings down, the stick transfers energy from the player's arms to the puck.

To shoot a slap shot, a hockey player draws back his stick, kind of like winding up a spring. A wind stores potential energy. When a player shoots, he converts potential energy into kinetic energy. He whips his stick down around toward the puck.

The stick bends when it makes contact with the puck. This is that winding-up-a-spring action again. It momentarily stores the energy created from the impact of the stick and puck.

The stick snaps forward, releasing that built up energy and flinging the puck forward.

The speed of a slap shot makes it difficult to stop. They can reach 100 miles (161 km) per hour, giving goalies a short time to react. But players sacrifice accuracy for speed with slap shots.

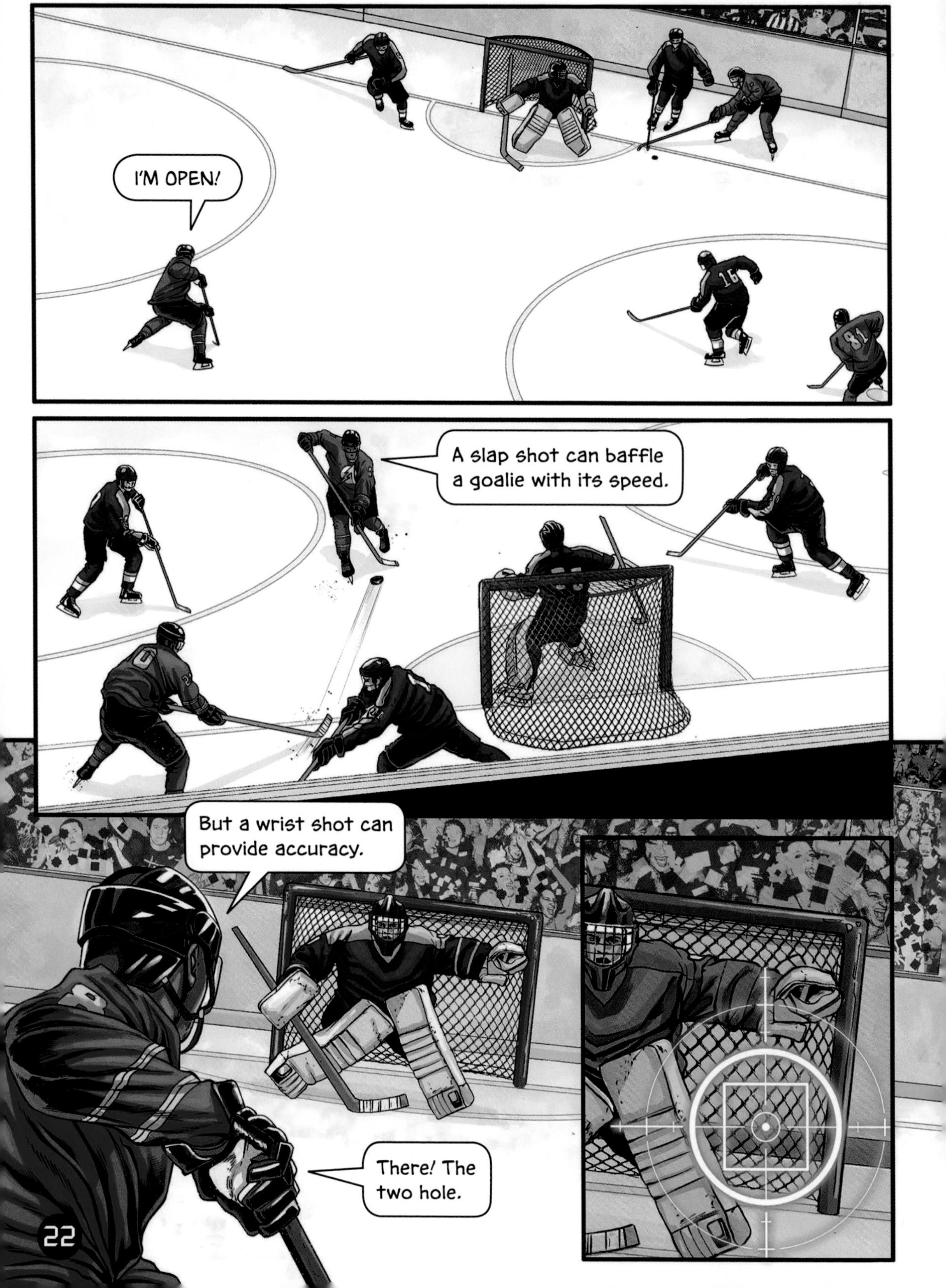
I'M OPEN!
16
81
A slap shot can baffle a goalie with its speed.
But a wrist shot can provide accuracy.
There! The two hole.

The tape on the blade rubs the side of the puck, creating a lot of friction. The puck doesn't simply slide off the blade. It begins to spin as the two surfaces try to hold onto each other.

Instead of bringing back my arms, I just bend my wrists back, like a smaller, less powerful spring. I will also keep the puck on my stick, which helps me aim better.

The spinning puck acts somewhat like a gyroscope to keep it flying in a straight line. A gyroscope is a wheel that spins inside a frame. The spinning causes the frame to balance in any position.

Yes!

23

Of course, it's not exactly easy scoring a goal.

Skillfully handling a puck and making shots gets easier with practice. But there is one player set on stopping the puck from getting into the net.

The goalie protects the net like a shield.

Oh no, it's a breakaway!

Let's use my special glasses to zoom in on this situation.

Goaltending is all about geometry. You need quick reactions to block a speeding puck. But by playing the angles, you can improve your odds of stopping a shot.

At best, the goalie's body blocks about 60 percent of the goal. That leaves a lot of room for a speeding puck to slip by.

By stepping out of the goal a couple of feet the goalie reduces the area open to a shot.

Save!

But a player trying to score can use this angle game too.

A player can use other players' bodies to block the goalie's line of sight.

The goalie has to find the right angle to see the puck while not leaving too much of the goal open.

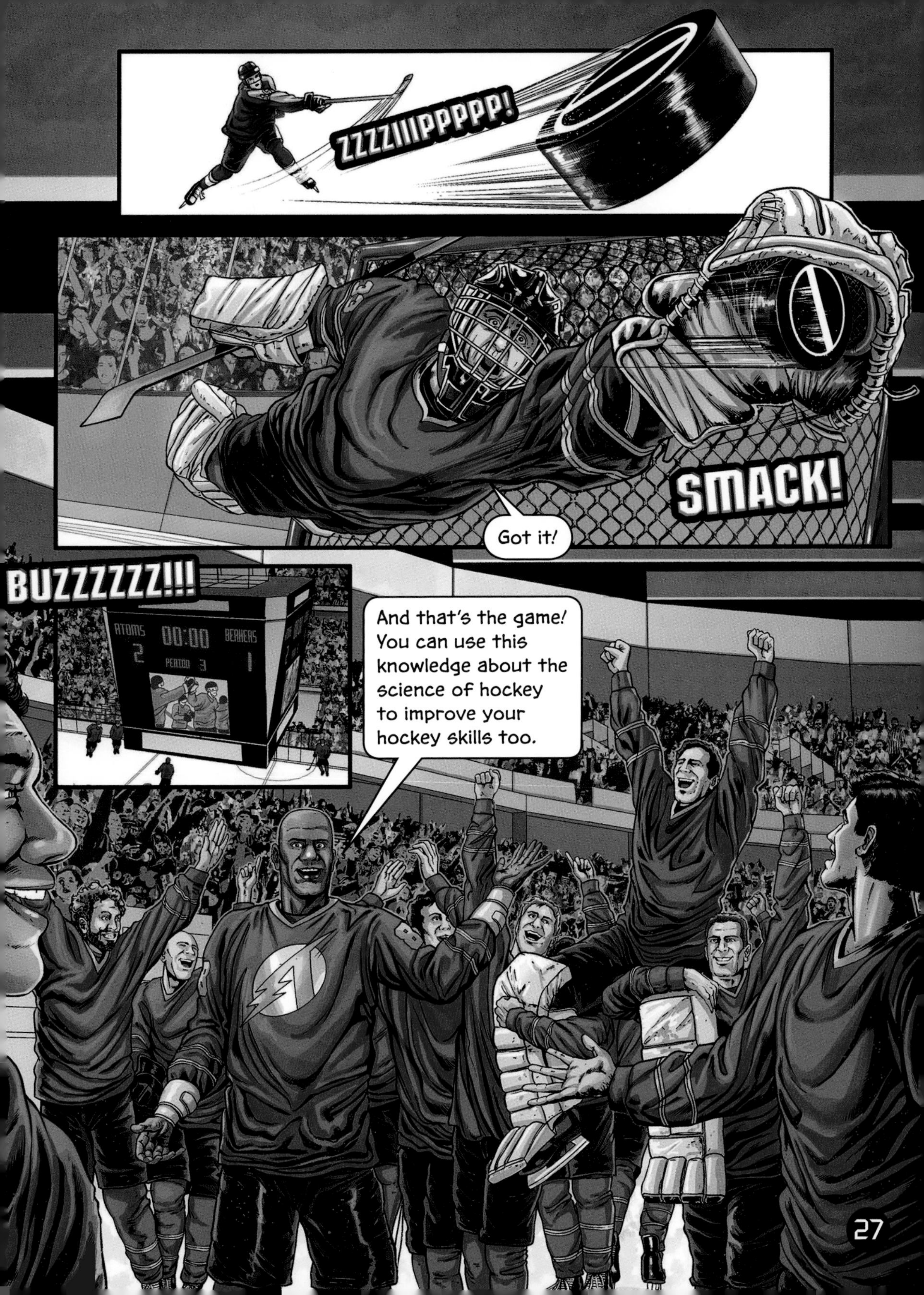
ZZZZIIIPPPPP!
SMACK!
Got it!
BUZZZZZZ!!!
ATOMS 00:00 BEAKERS
2 PERIOD 3 1
And that's the game! You can use this knowledge about the science of hockey to improve your hockey skills too.

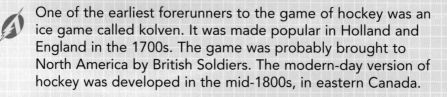

One of the earliest forerunners to the game of hockey was an ice game called kolven. It was made popular in Holland and England in the 1700s. The game was probably brought to North America by British Soldiers. The modern-day version of hockey was developed in the mid-1800s, in eastern Canada.

The first hockey rules were written by students at McGill University in Montreal, Canada. These students must have known what they were doing. Hockey's original rules have not changed much over the years. One major change involved decreasing the number of players per team from nine to six.

Hockey sticks were once only made of wood. But today, lighter and more durable materials—such as fiberglass and graphite—are also used.

Some of the first pucks weren't actually rubber disks, but rubber balls. They were hard to control as they bounced, instead of slid, on the ice. They often bounced out of the rink, endangering fans. Sometimes these balls were cut in half. Other pucks were made of wood.

The Stanley Cup is the world's oldest sports trophy. It was first awarded to the Montreal Amateur Athletic Association in 1893.

Hockey was first introduced to the Olympics in 1920. Canada won the gold medal that year. Canadian teams have won more Olympic gold medals (9 men's and 4 women's) than any other national hockey team.

The International Ice Hockey Federation (IIHF) was founded in 1908. It governs how the sport is played internationally. The IIHF has 73 member countries. Each country competes for one of 12 qualifying spots for men's teams and eight for women's teams in the Olympics.

 Between 12,000 and 15,000 gallons (45,425 and 56,781 liters) of water are used to form a hockey rink surface.

MORE ABOUT

SUPER SCIENTIST

Real name: Maxwell J. Axiom
Hometown: Seattle, Washington
Height: 6' 1"   Weight: 192 lbs
Eyes: Brown   Hair: None

Super capabilities: Super intelligence; able to shrink to the size of an atom; sunglasses give x-ray vision; lab coat allows for travel through time and space.

Origin: Since birth, Max Axiom seemed destined for greatness. His mother, a marine biologist, taught her son about the mysteries of the sea. His father, a nuclear physicist and volunteer park ranger, schooled Max on the wonders of earth and sky.

One day on a wilderness hike, a megacharged lightning bolt struck Max with blinding fury. When he awoke, Max discovered a newfound energy and set out to learn as much about science as possible. He traveled the globe earning degrees in every aspect of the field. Upon his return, he was ready to share his knowledge and new identity with the world. He had become Max Axiom, Super Scientist.

GLOSSARY

durable (DUR-uh-buhl)—able to last a long time

flexible (FLEHK-suh-buhl)—able to bend

friction (FRIK-shuhn)—the force of resistance created when two objects rub against each other

gyroscope (JEYE-ruh-skohp)—a spinning wheel or disk on an axis

kinetic energy (ki-NET-ik EN-ur-jee)—the energy produced by a moving object

molecule (MOL-uh-kyool)—a group of atoms; a molecule is the smallest amount of a substance

potential energy (puh-TEN-shuhl EN-ur-jee)—energy stored within an object, waiting to be released

quasi (KWAH-zee)—having some but not all of the features of something else

solid (SOL-id)—a substance with tightly packed molecules, not a gas or a liquid

traction (TRAK-shuhn)—the amount of grip one surface has while moving over another surface

vulcanized (VUHL-kuh-neyezd)—hardened and strengthened through a chemical process

READ MORE

Biskup, Agnieszka. *Hockey: How It Works.* The Science of Sports. North Mankato, Minn.: Capstone Press, 2010.

Frederick, Shane. *The Technology of Hockey.* High-Tech Sports. North Mankato, Minn.: Capstone Press, 2013.

Savage, Jeff. *Top 25 Hockey Skills, Tips, and Tricks.* Berkeley Heights, N.J.: Enslow Publishers, Inc., 2012.

Stuckey, Rachel. *Up Your Game On and Off the Ice.* Hockey Source. New York: Crabtree Publishing Company, 2015.

INTERNET SITES

FactHound offers a safe, fun way to find Internet sites related to this book. All sites on FactHound have been researched by our staff.

Here's all you do:

Visit *www.facthound.com*

Type in this code: 9781491460863

Check out projects, games and lots more at
www.capstonekids.com

INDEX

Bolt, Usain, 7

Davis, Shani, 7

friction, 6, 7, 9, 10, 19, 23

goalies, 13, 21, 22, 24, 25, 26
gyroscopes, 23

heat energy, 16
hockey rinks, 8, 11, 13, 28, 29
hockey sticks, 12, 18, 19, 20,
    21, 23, 28

ice, 4, 6, 7, 8, 9, 10, 11, 14,
    15, 16, 17, 18, 19, 20,
    28, 29
ice skates, 4, 7, 9, 10, 12, 13,
    14, 15, 18
International Ice Hockey
    Federation (IIHF), 29

kinetic energy, 20
kolven, 28

molecules, 9, 16, 17

Olympics, 28, 29

playing the angles, 25–26
potential energy, 20
pucks, 4, 8, 9, 12, 13, 16, 17,
    18, 19, 20, 21, 23, 24, 25,
    26, 28

quasi fluid, 9

safety equipment, 12–13
slap shots, 5, 19, 20, 21, 22
solids, 8, 9
speed skating, 7
Stanley Cup, 28

traction, 10

wrist shots, 22–23

Zamboni, 14–15